The Weekly Prep!
Planner

The Weekly Prep!
Planner

Copyright © 2022 by Nely Sanchez

ALL RIGHTS RESERVED

No part of this book may be reproduced, scanned, or transmitted in any form, or by any means whatsoever (electronic, mechanical, or otherwise) including photocopying, without the prior written permission and consent of the publisher, except where permitted by law.

Hardcover (Black): ISBN 13: 978-1-951137-16-8
Paperback (Black): ISBN 13: 978-1-951137-18-2
*
Hardcover (Blue): ISBN 13: 978-1-951137-20-5
Paperback (Blue): ISBN 13: 978-1-951137-21-2

BCLS Creative Publishing Group

This Book Belongs To:

_____

Email: _____

Cell: _____

Home: _____

~ Welcome to *The Weekly Prep!* ~

This is an undated one-year planner, so you can begin at any point in the year.

On the *weekly to-do pages*, choose an important core area or category in your life.

Example: Family, Business, School, Home

Underneath each category, write down the list of things you need to accomplish.

Example: Dental Appointments, Business Meetings, Travel Plans, Important Phone Calls

Schedule these must-do's into the *weekly time blocker*, along with your daily rituals.

Example: 5:00 a.m. to 6:00 a.m. – Personal Development

6:00 a.m. to 6:30 a.m. - Workout

There are blank monthly calendars for you to insert your important monthly events, as well as lined note pages at the end of the planner.

At the end of the week, transfer any uncompleted items forward, and plan a new week!

We hope that this little book will become an important companion to you in planning your life, dreams, and daily habits.

We sincerely wish you the best!

Month: _____

Sunday	Monday	Tuesday	Wednesday

Thursday	Friday	Saturday	Notes

Time Blocker

	Monday	Tuesday	Wednesday	Thursday	Friday	Saturday	Sunday
5							
6							
7							
8							
9							
10							
11							
12							
1							
2							
3							
4							
5							
6							
7							
8							

Weekly To-Do

Week of: _____

_____	_____
_____	_____
_____	_____

Time Blocker

	Monday	Tuesday	Wednesday	Thursday	Friday	Saturday	Sunday
5							
6							
7							
8							
9							
10							
11							
12							
1							
2							
3							
4							
5							
6							
7							
8							

Weekly To-Do

Week of: _____

Time Blocker

	Monday	Tuesday	Wednesday	Thursday	Friday	Saturday	Sunday
5							
6							
7							
8							
9							
10							
11							
12							
1							
2							
3							
4							
5							
6							
7							
8							

Weekly To-Do

Week of: _____

Time Blocker

	Monday	Tuesday	Wednesday	Thursday	Friday	Saturday	Sunday
5							
6							
7							
8							
9							
10							
11							
12							
1							
2							
3							
4							
5							
6							
7							
8							

Weekly To-Do

Week of: _____

Time Blocker

	Monday	Tuesday	Wednesday	Thursday	Friday	Saturday	Sunday
5							
6							
7							
8							
9							
10							
11							
12							
1							
2							
3							
4							
5							
6							
7							
8							

Weekly To-Do

Week of: _____

_____	_____

_____	_____

_____	_____

*Month:*_____

Sunday	Monday	Tuesday	Wednesday

Thursday	Friday	Saturday	Notes

Time Blocker

	Monday	Tuesday	Wednesday	Thursday	Friday	Saturday	Sunday
5							
6							
7							
8							
9							
10							
11							
12							
1							
2							
3							
4							
5							
6							
7							
8							

Weekly To-Do

Week of: _____

Time Blocker

	Monday	Tuesday	Wednesday	Thursday	Friday	Saturday	Sunday
5							
6							
7							
8							
9							
10							
11							
12							
1							
2							
3							
4							
5							
6							
7							
8							

Weekly To-Do

Week of: _____

Time Blocker

	Monday	Tuesday	Wednesday	Thursday	Friday	Saturday	Sunday
5							
6							
7							
8							
9							
10							
11							
12							
1							
2							
3							
4							
5							
6							
7							
8							

Weekly To-Do

Week of: _____

Time Blocker

	Monday	Tuesday	Wednesday	Thursday	Friday	Saturday	Sunday
5							
6							
7							
8							
9							
10							
11							
12							
1							
2							
3							
4							
5							
6							
7							
8							

Weekly To-Do

Week of: _____

Time Blocker

	Monday	Tuesday	Wednesday	Thursday	Friday	Saturday	Sunday
5							
6							
7							
8							
9							
10							
11							
12							
1							
2							
3							
4							
5							
6							
7							
8							

Weekly To-Do

Week of: _____

Month: _____

Sunday	Monday	Tuesday	Wednesday

Thursday	Friday	Saturday	Notes

Time Blocker

	Monday	Tuesday	Wednesday	Thursday	Friday	Saturday	Sunday
5							
6							
7							
8							
9							
10							
11							
12							
1							
2							
3							
4							
5							
6							
7							
8							

Weekly To-Do

Week of: _____

Time Blocker

	Monday	Tuesday	Wednesday	Thursday	Friday	Saturday	Sunday
5							
6							
7							
8							
9							
10							
11							
12							
1							
2							
3							
4							
5							
6							
7							
8							

Weekly To-Do

Week of: _____

Time Blocker

	Monday	Tuesday	Wednesday	Thursday	Friday	Saturday	Sunday
5							
6							
7							
8							
9							
10							
11							
12							
1							
2							
3							
4							
5							
6							
7							
8							

Weekly To-Do

Week of: _____

Time Blocker

	Monday	Tuesday	Wednesday	Thursday	Friday	Saturday	Sunday
5							
6							
7							
8							
9							
10							
11							
12							
1							
2							
3							
4							
5							
6							
7							
8							

Weekly To-Do

Week of: _____

Time Blocker

	Monday	Tuesday	Wednesday	Thursday	Friday	Saturday	Sunday
5							
6							
7							
8							
9							
10							
11							
12							
1							
2							
3							
4							
5							
6							
7							
8							

Weekly To-Do

Week of: _____

Month: _____

Sunday	Monday	Tuesday	Wednesday

Thursday	Friday	Saturday	Notes

Time Blocker

	Monday	Tuesday	Wednesday	Thursday	Friday	Saturday	Sunday
5							
6							
7							
8							
9							
10							
11							
12							
1							
2							
3							
4							
5							
6							
7							
8							

Weekly To-Do

Week of: _____

Time Blocker

	Monday	Tuesday	Wednesday	Thursday	Friday	Saturday	Sunday
5							
6							
7							
8							
9							
10							
11							
12							
1							
2							
3							
4							
5							
6							
7							
8							

Weekly To-Do

Week of: _____

Time Blocker

	Monday	Tuesday	Wednesday	Thursday	Friday	Saturday	Sunday
5							
6							
7							
8							
9							
10							
11							
12							
1							
2							
3							
4							
5							
6							
7							
8							

Weekly To-Do

Week of: _____

Time Blocker

	Monday	Tuesday	Wednesday	Thursday	Friday	Saturday	Sunday
5							
6							
7							
8							
9							
10							
11							
12							
1							
2							
3							
4							
5							
6							
7							
8							

Weekly To-Do

Week of: _____

Time Blocker

	Monday	Tuesday	Wednesday	Thursday	Friday	Saturday	Sunday
5							
6							
7							
8							
9							
10							
11							
12							
1							
2							
3							
4							
5							
6							
7							
8							

Weekly To-Do

Week of: _____

Month:_____

Sunday	Monday	Tuesday	Wednesday

Thursday	Friday	Saturday	Notes

Time Blocker

	Monday	Tuesday	Wednesday	Thursday	Friday	Saturday	Sunday
5							
6							
7							
8							
9							
10							
11							
12							
1							
2							
3							
4							
5							
6							
7							
8							

Weekly To-Do

Week of: _____

Time Blocker

	Monday	Tuesday	Wednesday	Thursday	Friday	Saturday	Sunday
5							
6							
7							
8							
9							
10							
11							
12							
1							
2							
3							
4							
5							
6							
7							
8							

Weekly To-Do

Week of: _____

Time Blocker

	Monday	Tuesday	Wednesday	Thursday	Friday	Saturday	Sunday
5							
6							
7							
8							
9							
10							
11							
12							
1							
2							
3							
4							
5							
6							
7							
8							

Weekly To-Do

Week of: _____

Time Blocker

	Monday	Tuesday	Wednesday	Thursday	Friday	Saturday	Sunday
5							
6							
7							
8							
9							
10							
11							
12							
1							
2							
3							
4							
5							
6							
7							
8							

Weekly To-Do

Week of: _____

Time Blocker

	Monday	Tuesday	Wednesday	Thursday	Friday	Saturday	Sunday
5							
6							
7							
8							
9							
10							
11							
12							
1							
2							
3							
4							
5							
6							
7							
8							

Weekly To-Do

Week of: _____

Month: _____

Sunday	Monday	Tuesday	Wednesday

Thursday	Friday	Saturday	Notes

Time Blocker

	Monday	Tuesday	Wednesday	Thursday	Friday	Saturday	Sunday
5							
6							
7							
8							
9							
10							
11							
12							
1							
2							
3							
4							
5							
6							
7							
8							

Weekly To-Do

Week of: _____

Time Blocker

	Monday	Tuesday	Wednesday	Thursday	Friday	Saturday	Sunday
5							
6							
7							
8							
9							
10							
11							
12							
1							
2							
3							
4							
5							
6							
7							
8							

Weekly To-Do

Week of: _____

Time Blocker

	Monday	Tuesday	Wednesday	Thursday	Friday	Saturday	Sunday
5							
6							
7							
8							
9							
10							
11							
12							
1							
2							
3							
4							
5							
6							
7							
8							

Weekly To-Do

Week of: _____

Time Blocker

	Monday	Tuesday	Wednesday	Thursday	Friday	Saturday	Sunday
5							
6							
7							
8							
9							
10							
11							
12							
1							
2							
3							
4							
5							
6							
7							
8							

Weekly To-Do

Week of: _____

Time Blocker

	Monday	Tuesday	Wednesday	Thursday	Friday	Saturday	Sunday
5							
6							
7							
8							
9							
10							
11							
12							
1							
2							
3							
4							
5							
6							
7							
8							

Weekly To-Do

Week of: _____

Month:

Sunday	Monday	Tuesday	Wednesday

Thursday	Friday	Saturday	Notes

Time Blocker

	Monday	Tuesday	Wednesday	Thursday	Friday	Saturday	Sunday
5							
6							
7							
8							
9							
10							
11							
12							
1							
2							
3							
4							
5							
6							
7							
8							

Weekly To-Do

Week of: _____

Time Blocker

	Monday	Tuesday	Wednesday	Thursday	Friday	Saturday	Sunday
5							
6							
7							
8							
9							
10							
11							
12							
1							
2							
3							
4							
5							
6							
7							
8							

Weekly To-Do

Week of: _____

Time Blocker

	Monday	Tuesday	Wednesday	Thursday	Friday	Saturday	Sunday
5							
6							
7							
8							
9							
10							
11							
12							
1							
2							
3							
4							
5							
6							
7							
8							

Weekly To-Do

Week of: _____

Time Blocker

	Monday	Tuesday	Wednesday	Thursday	Friday	Saturday	Sunday
5							
6							
7							
8							
9							
10							
11							
12							
1							
2							
3							
4							
5							
6							
7							
8							

Weekly To-Do

Week of: _____

Time Blocker

	Monday	Tuesday	Wednesday	Thursday	Friday	Saturday	Sunday
5							
6							
7							
8							
9							
10							
11							
12							
1							
2							
3							
4							
5							
6							
7							
8							

Weekly To-Do

Week of: _____

Month:_____

Sunday	Monday	Tuesday	Wednesday

Thursday	Friday	Saturday	Notes

Time Blocker

	Monday	Tuesday	Wednesday	Thursday	Friday	Saturday	Sunday
5							
6							
7							
8							
9							
10							
11							
12							
1							
2							
3							
4							
5							
6							
7							
8							

Weekly To-Do

Week of: _____

Time Blocker

	Monday	Tuesday	Wednesday	Thursday	Friday	Saturday	Sunday
5							
6							
7							
8							
9							
10							
11							
12							
1							
2							
3							
4							
5							
6							
7							
8							

Weekly To-Do

Week of: _____

Time Blocker

	Monday	Tuesday	Wednesday	Thursday	Friday	Saturday	Sunday
5							
6							
7							
8							
9							
10							
11							
12							
1							
2							
3							
4							
5							
6							
7							
8							

Weekly To-Do

Week of: _____

Time Blocker

	Monday	Tuesday	Wednesday	Thursday	Friday	Saturday	Sunday
5							
6							
7							
8							
9							
10							
11							
12							
1							
2							
3							
4							
5							
6							
7							
8							

Weekly To-Do

Week of: _____

Time Blocker

	Monday	Tuesday	Wednesday	Thursday	Friday	Saturday	Sunday
5							
6							
7							
8							
9							
10							
11							
12							
1							
2							
3							
4							
5							
6							
7							
8							

Weekly To-Do

Week of: _____

Month:_____

Sunday	Monday	Tuesday	Wednesday

Thursday	Friday	Saturday	Notes

Time Blocker

	Monday	Tuesday	Wednesday	Thursday	Friday	Saturday	Sunday
5							
6							
7							
8							
9							
10							
11							
12							
1							
2							
3							
4							
5							
6							
7							
8							

Weekly To-Do

Week of: _____

Time Blocker

	Monday	Tuesday	Wednesday	Thursday	Friday	Saturday	Sunday
5							
6							
7							
8							
9							
10							
11							
12							
1							
2							
3							
4							
5							
6							
7							
8							

Weekly To-Do

Week of: _____

_____	_____

_____	_____

_____	_____

Time Blocker

	Monday	Tuesday	Wednesday	Thursday	Friday	Saturday	Sunday
5							
6							
7							
8							
9							
10							
11							
12							
1							
2							
3							
4							
5							
6							
7							
8							

Weekly To-Do

Week of: _____

Time Blocker

	Monday	Tuesday	Wednesday	Thursday	Friday	Saturday	Sunday
5							
6							
7							
8							
9							
10							
11							
12							
1							
2							
3							
4							
5							
6							
7							
8							

Weekly To-Do

Week of: _____

Time Blocker

	Monday	Tuesday	Wednesday	Thursday	Friday	Saturday	Sunday
5							
6							
7							
8							
9							
10							
11							
12							
1							
2							
3							
4							
5							
6							
7							
8							

Weekly To-Do

Week of: _____

Month: _____

Sunday	Monday	Tuesday	Wednesday

Thursday	Friday	Saturday	Notes

Time Blocker

	Monday	Tuesday	Wednesday	Thursday	Friday	Saturday	Sunday
5							
6							
7							
8							
9							
10							
11							
12							
1							
2							
3							
4							
5							
6							
7							
8							

Weekly To-Do

Week of: _____

Time Blocker

	Monday	Tuesday	Wednesday	Thursday	Friday	Saturday	Sunday
5							
6							
7							
8							
9							
10							
11							
12							
1							
2							
3							
4							
5							
6							
7							
8							

Weekly To-Do

Week of: _____

Time Blocker

	Monday	Tuesday	Wednesday	Thursday	Friday	Saturday	Sunday
5							
6							
7							
8							
9							
10							
11							
12							
1							
2							
3							
4							
5							
6							
7							
8							

Weekly To-Do

Week of: _____

Time Blocker

	Monday	Tuesday	Wednesday	Thursday	Friday	Saturday	Sunday
5							
6							
7							
8							
9							
10							
11							
12							
1							
2							
3							
4							
5							
6							
7							
8							

Weekly To-Do

Week of: _____

Time Blocker

	Monday	Tuesday	Wednesday	Thursday	Friday	Saturday	Sunday
5							
6							
7							
8							
9							
10							
11							
12							
1							
2							
3							
4							
5							
6							
7							
8							

Weekly To-Do

Week of: _____

Month:_____

Sunday	Monday	Tuesday	Wednesday

Thursday	Friday	Saturday	Notes

Time Blocker

	Monday	Tuesday	Wednesday	Thursday	Friday	Saturday	Sunday
5							
6							
7							
8							
9							
10							
11							
12							
1							
2							
3							
4							
5							
6							
7							
8							

Weekly To-Do

Week of: _____

Time Blocker

	Monday	Tuesday	Wednesday	Thursday	Friday	Saturday	Sunday
5							
6							
7							
8							
9							
10							
11							
12							
1							
2							
3							
4							
5							
6							
7							
8							

Weekly To-Do

Week of: _____

Time Blocker

	Monday	Tuesday	Wednesday	Thursday	Friday	Saturday	Sunday
5							
6							
7							
8							
9							
10							
11							
12							
1							
2							
3							
4							
5							
6							
7							
8							

Weekly To-Do

Week of: _____

Time Blocker

	Monday	Tuesday	Wednesday	Thursday	Friday	Saturday	Sunday
5							
6							
7							
8							
9							
10							
11							
12							
1							
2							
3							
4							
5							
6							
7							
8							

Weekly To-Do

Week of: _____

Time Blocker

	Monday	Tuesday	Wednesday	Thursday	Friday	Saturday	Sunday
5							
6							
7							
8							
9							
10							
11							
12							
1							
2							
3							
4							
5							
6							
7							
8							

Weekly To-Do

Week of: _____

Month: _____

Sunday	Monday	Tuesday	Wednesday

Thursday	Friday	Saturday	Notes

Time Blocker

	Monday	Tuesday	Wednesday	Thursday	Friday	Saturday	Sunday
5							
6							
7							
8							
9							
10							
11							
12							
1							
2							
3							
4							
5							
6							
7							
8							

Weekly To-Do

Week of: _____

_____	_____

_____	_____

_____	_____

Time Blocker

	Monday	Tuesday	Wednesday	Thursday	Friday	Saturday	Sunday
5							
6							
7							
8							
9							
10							
11							
12							
1							
2							
3							
4							
5							
6							
7							
8							

Weekly To-Do

Week of: _____

Time Blocker

	Monday	Tuesday	Wednesday	Thursday	Friday	Saturday	Sunday
5							
6							
7							
8							
9							
10							
11							
12							
1							
2							
3							
4							
5							
6							
7							
8							

Weekly To-Do

Week of: _____

Time Blocker

	Monday	Tuesday	Wednesday	Thursday	Friday	Saturday	Sunday
5							
6							
7							
8							
9							
10							
11							
12							
1							
2							
3							
4							
5							
6							
7							
8							

Weekly To-Do

Week of: _____

Time Blocker

	Monday	Tuesday	Wednesday	Thursday	Friday	Saturday	Sunday
5							
6							
7							
8							
9							
10							
11							
12							
1							
2							
3							
4							
5							
6							
7							
8							

Weekly To-Do

Week of: _____

Notes

Notes

Notes

Notes

www.ingramcontent.com/pod-product-compliance
Lightning Source LLC
Chambersburg PA
CBHW080457240426
43673CB00005B/214